FIFTEEN FIRST TIMES

BEGINNINGS: A COLLECTION OF INDELIBLE FIRSTS

D.G. KAYE

Trade Paperback Release: December 2022
ISBN: 978-0-9947938-8-1 Paperback

Electronic book edition published 2022.

Book layout by *Moyhill*.

Also Written by D.G. Kaye

Twenty Years: After "I Do"
P.S. I Forgive You
Conflicted Hearts
Words We Carry
Have Bags, Will Travel
MenoWhat? A Memoir

Disclaimer

Fifteen First Times is a work of nonfiction. This book was written according to the author's recollection of events in her life. Some names have been changed or omitted in order to maintain the anonymity of those mentioned. Any medical and financial references in this book are made solely from the author's experience, and she advises her readers to always seek medical and financial advice to suit their own individual needs.

Acknowledgments

This book was a wonderful reminiscence of the past. It has been a few years since I've put out a new book because a lot of life was happening—and not happening through that span of time.

My heartfelt thanks to all of you who have helped me through the troubled journey I've been on for the past two years—keeping my spirit alive in the writing world when I had no words. I'd especially like to thank my dear friend and short story writer extraordinaire, author Sally Cronin, for her love and support throughout my journey. And I would also like to thank my dear spiritual sister author Tina Frisco, for her compassion and intense beta reading, and most valuable feedback, and Colleen Chesebro, of Unicorn Cats Publishing, for her creativity and original book cover design.

Contents

Dedication

To those who've been there, done that, and learned from. And for those who've yet to venture out and overcome.

Thoughts

Do you ever think back on past events which have left an indelible impression on you or your life, or find that the incidents you've endured through life have helped shape the person you've become? Are your formed perceptions and values developed from experience, and have they consequently become incorporated into your daily life? Our experiences are steppingstones for much of what feeds our character. We live, we experience, we learn, we become, and we overcome.

Nobody sent me the memo on life, and most of the time, I had zero confidence to broach the subject of my conflictions and situations with anyone. All these events I experienced and share in my stories happened with little to no guidance or knowledge, making much of my young life experiences processes of trial and error. I was like the proverbial child who grew up in the wild, except I had parents and a comfortable home.

In these fifteen short stories, I'm fessing up to some firsts in my life, some of which turned out to serve as monumental lessons. These weren't life-altering moments, but rather, moments of teaching to move my life forward, leaving me with scars and awakening moments, confirming my curiosities, and leading me in new directions of growth.

Crazy Diets

I'm not sure what conjured up these memories—maybe a book I read or perhaps something I took from reading many blogs on health and wellness. Whatever stirred up these memories, brought to mind when I first became self-conscious about my appearance, what I disliked about myself, and my growing desire to fix my flaws—all of which led to my first diet at a young age.

As a little girl who always admired anything and everyone beautiful, I soon began paying attention to my own outward appearance. I was a plain-looking child with long, stick-straight blonde hair and almond-shaped green eyes. My eyes were the only pretty feature I inherited from my mother. The blonde came from my fair-haired father. Besides these two redeeming features, I never thought I looked like anyone in my family—until later in life. My weight was yet to be a concerning factor for me, and I didn't yet understand the concept about fattening foods or nutritional health. Although my already fashion-conscious-self developed early, around the age of seven or eight, I wasn't yet familiar with the term 'fat'.

By the time I was approaching twelve years old, I'd noticed a few 'calorie counter' booklets lying around on my mother's nightstand. By this time my mother was already a long-time diet freak, but I didn't discover just how crazy her dieting really was until another few years had passed, and I heard whispers of *diet pills*—which I learned later were the culprits for some of her maniacal moments. But I was newly becoming aware of how my body was changing, and my Aunty Sherry, who was staying with us during that time, was the one looking out for me during my transformation to womanhood.

I'd never considered my mother or my aunt *fat* or even overweight, but I became curious about this new *diet* business as my blue jeans began to feel as though they were shrinking on me, even after I'd stopped putting them in the dryer. I was twelve when I had my first *real* boyfriend (as you will learn about in a later chapter), and all those McDonald's chocolate milkshakes and fries were causing the extra ten pounds that enjoyed living on my hips and thighs.

My Aunty Sherry was the first person to lift my self-esteem. She'd always tell me I was beautiful and *voluptuous* because I had a tiny waist and curvy hips. That may sound sexy to some, but for me, at 5' 3" and very short-waisted, I felt as though my hips were so close to my boobs that they were practically conjoined. And after snooping into those calorie-counting booklets, I summoned the courage to ask my aunt how the diet thing worked. I was starting from scratch, learning about how to count calories to lose weight.

I was never much of a big eater, and less of one now, but I thrived on junk food for most of my childhood and teens—save for the times I was dieting. In our home, corn and potatoes were the only vegetables we were familiar with. The only exercise I took was the two-mile walk back and forth to junior high school, and later, the one-mile walk to the bus stop, where I'd change buses three times to get to high school. The brand-new Golden Arches opened, conveniently, in front of the bus stop. It was comforting and convenient for me to pick up a chocolate milkshake and French fries to accompany me on my fifteen-minute walk home. Treats were my comfort foods to help quash all the emotional wounds I harbored growing up in my dysfunctional home life.

The diets became an on-and-off interlude. Over time, I learned how many calories were in every food. Since then and till this day, I learned to keep a mental tally of my daily intake of calories. And after all those crazy years, my count is now more concerned with carbs. Menopause and carbs didn't play nicely together. I digress, but there were plenty of kooky diets being followed back in the day. Nobody in my family was what I considered *fat*, and I sure didn't want to be the one to lead the way. But I did.

My distracting home life had me becoming a frequent fridge visitor, particularly late at night when nobody was around to police me. I'd developed some strange cravings. Dunking chocolate chip cookies in milk was my go-to, but it wasn't strange to find me digging into a mayonnaise jar with a spoon either. The ketchup chips and chocolate bars were my mainstay comfort foods.

The diets! Let's recap: the egg diet, the banana diet, the grapefruit diet, the cabbage soup diet, the Atkins diet, the Dr. Bernstein diet (craziest of all, but I'll get back to that one later), and the most popular and considered the healthiest of these diets was the Diet Workshop diet, which had similar elements to the Weight Watchers diet, except there was no point system. The basis of Diet Workshop then, was a calorie-based diet with measured foods. And oh yes, I was a full-fledged member of the Diet Workshop club, because my Aunty Sherry joined us up. Diets were an ongoing exploration for both my mother and aunt in those days, despite their often not requiring to be on a diet.

Picking a diet was easy with so many choices—but sticking to them became another entity all together and maintaining the weight-loss was another whole issue. I was always game to start, I followed religiously, and I even lost weight—often, because of the number of times I stopped and started. My midnight visits to the fridge were my self-sabotage. But I was a champion at starting over—and over.

My teen years continued with my sampling of the various diets, until the sight of an egg, banana, grapefruit, or cabbage nauseated me to death—especially bananas. I hated them before I even lived on them for a week or two at a time. The Atkins diet consisted mostly of meat, eggs, and fat—with a smattering of low-carb, non-starch vegetables till my heart's content, but nothing else. Oh sure, I lost weight on that diet, but I also got sick—no surprise how hard my liver had to work with my mainly ingesting so much protein. So, the years rolled by, with several diets of lost and gained pounds; and by the time I was seventeen, this petite girl was pushing into a size fourteen! I couldn't stand myself. But no fears! Mother to the rescue with the newfound diet she'd learned about from her gossip sessions with girlfriends. The Dr. Bernstein diet was the newest craze, and it wasn't cheap!

That then-new diet was comparable to the new ketogenic diets of today—low carb, high protein, and no high glycemic vegetables. It was expensive, but if you followed it to the letter—living on a meager 800-900 calories per day and driving to the clinic a few days a week to get *the shot*—advertisements stated one could lose quite a bit of weight in less time, compared with a more balanced and diversified diet. *The shot,* said to be a concoction of vitamins B6, B12, and possibly other goodies, was part of the package to assist in breaking down fat faster.

My father was eager and happy to pay for me to go on this diet, as he would have done anything to make me happy. And by that point in my life, my weight was depressing me. I lost thirty-five pounds in less than three months. I became a size five! Just as my new body developed, my social life began to bloom. I went downtown to nightclubs with friends, feeling fantabulous, until approximately four-five months later—when I had incrementally gained back ALL the weight plus fifteen more pounds! NOBODY had taught me about *follow-up* maintenance plans! My new bod was short-lived.

My diet failure concerned me most when my father signed me up for a six-week tour of Israel and four countries in Europe, for my eighteenth birthday gift. (Some of that trip is featured here later.) I was the biggest I'd ever been by then, a tight size sixteen, but I had the time of my life. And seven months later, I moved away from home.

Moving away from home turned out to be my sanity in life in so many ways. I was physically free from my mother, experiencing and living life with no boundaries. I made new friends, worked part time, went to university part time, but best of all, before another year had passed, I'd lost back all the weight on my own—counting calories! I dieted at a steady pace of my own, without everyone else's rules, having nobody to report to, and had more success with no longer living in a stressful environment. The magic number was 1000. Eat whatever I wanted, providing I didn't go over 1000 calories daily. If I was going partying, I learned to save room in the count for a few glasses of wine, which was much more important than food at the time, lol. I made deals with myself and sacrificed for the things I enjoyed. Before my twentieth birthday I was a comfortable size six/seven for the rest of my days—until menopause hit, but I already wrote a book about that.

I found as the years and the newfangled diets passed, it was the old standbys that were the best diets. Diet Workshop (like Weight Watchers) was one of the best, because it offered a healthy eating plan that included all food groups, didn't deny the body of essential nutrients, and had a plan for sensible eating. This plan enabled me to lose approximately two to three pounds per week, in between the plateaus. I learned well that fast weight loss fad diets were unsustainable, and slow and steady, becoming a lifestyle change, rather than a diet, was the best way to lose and maintain. Most importantly, I learned that all fad diets require disciplined maintenance if there is any hope of keeping the weight off.

These days, I still do a mental count of everything that goes into my mouth. I've found that carbs were stubborn culprits after I turned fifty and began focusing more on them as the baddies than the calories. I learned what the dreaded *muffin top* meant without so much as changing the lifestyle diet that worked for me since I was twenty. I think as we age, the body retaliates for all the sins committed in the name of fat and Yo-Yo dieting. Without changing a thing, our body reallocates and shifts our weight without us inviting it to. Middle-age spread is not a myth. I compare it to an old pair of pants that eventually stretch out over time. The pants may have begun at a certain size, but they take on a whole new relaxed shape as they mold to our body changes.

I still fight back, disciplining myself daily, knowing I must keep fit. It doesn't get easier with age, but I will fight to defend what I've worked so hard to keep under control most of my life—even if the dreaded menopause dragons tested my limits and miraculously turned my hard-earned size six body into an eight.

For the Love of Shoes

I was three.

I must have been a shoe or did something related to shoes in another life because I proudly own up to becoming a shoe-a-holic in this life. My memories of ogling and desiring to wear high heels go back to when I was three years old, according to my *shoe love* stories from my mother and aunt. My mother dubbed me a shoe menace when she'd take me with her to her beauty parlor appointments.

The story goes, I had quite an attraction for pretty shoes. After my mother had her hair dyed and set in rollers, she'd join the other ladies of leisure under the hair dryers, where some took to gossip while others took advantage of the respite and snoozed. What was a barely yet four-year-old to do to keep herself busy?

I was a crafty child, even at three. According to my mother (I always took her stories with a grain of salt until verified by my aunt), I took focus on the *sleeping* ladies. My attraction to towering heels fed my admiration with curiosity, so what harm was there in removing shoes from sleeping women and strutting up and down the salon in them? But the fun ended when my mother's roving eye would awaken to do a spot check on me. She'd instruct me to put the shoes back on the ladies' feet every time I went back for another try. According to this lore, that hobby of mine was far from a one-time gig. But the women laughed and thought I was adorable.

Apparently, I wasn't choosy about the shoes I pinched so long as they had heels. Shoes were far more entertaining for my imagination than toys. My shoe passion continues to this day. The first memories of my passion for shoes began at home. My mother had a beautiful collection of stilettos. In fact, she had so many that several pairs remained in our basement because they couldn't all fit in her closet. And sadly, it appears this little peach didn't fall far from the shoe tree. The little shoe haven in the basement gave me such pleasure and imaginative ideas. Nobody frequented the basement except for laundry time, making it the perfect playroom for me to strut around playing house, bride, and movie star, my favorite imaginary games where I was the featured character in all. I knew that movie stars, brides, and fancy moms all wore beautiful stilettos.

I'm not exactly clear on where my obsession came from—other than my love of all things beautiful—but my compulsion never faded, although my tastes have varied through the years, as the shoe count kept escalating. Prancing around with the clickety-clack of the heels hitting the ground gave off a lyrical sound to my ears.

Despite my admitted addiction to shoes, I find it hilarious when looking back on those shoe-inspired memories and owning up to my silliness. Who can say where creativity or passions come from? Many of my make-believe moments were solo events, as my sister was yet to be born and my two brothers shared no love for my passion. Funny enough, my sister and I are complete opposites in more ways than one. She never got the shoe bug, and to this day prefers flip flops or sneakers to heels.

I rebelled against *kiddie* shoes my entire childhood. I wanted to wear grown-up shoes. The 1960s burst with Saddle shoes, but I hated them. I wanted party shoes! That's how I referred to shiny black patent leather shoes with bows and slightly elevated heels. I loved bows. But sadly, party shoes were only for special occasions—and wearing around the house when nobody was around. I still remember my first black patent leather party shoes my father bought me, complete with bows. I couldn't have been more than five or six years old. He took me to a shoe store one Saturday afternoon on one of his visitation weekends and bought me the most beautiful shoes I thought I'd ever seen. I can still remember the excitement I felt sliding my feet into my very own grown-up-looking shoes, and the heartache I later endured as my feet continued to grow and they no longer fit.

I still don't know what sparked my obsession with shoes, other than the visual appeal and the clacking sound they made when the heels hit the ground playing a short symphony to my ears with every consecutive step. No doubt, a Saddle shoe or sneaker couldn't match this excitement. I wasn't any different from any other kid who couldn't wait to become a grown up, but my reasons differed from most kids.

Even the sound of my grandmother's orthopedic shoes intrigued me. When she'd take us for walks down her cobblestone street and the metal taps on the bottom of her shoes touched the pavement with every step, it sounded like the hooves of a Clydesdale horse landing on pavement as it galloped. The sound of her shoes intrigued me, but I had no desire to try them on. I may have been only five or six at the time, but one thing was certain—I didn't want to wear *grandmother* shoes!

Then one day while snooping through her back closet looking for something to entertain myself with, to my surprise and delight, I came across a box stashed far back on a shelf. When I realized it was a shoebox, there was no stopping me from looking inside.

My excitement mounted upon the discovery of a beautiful pair of turquoise satin stilettos. Even as a child I found it puzzling to find that my grandmother had those shoes, let alone that she had worn them. I didn't hesitate to ask her if they were hers and why I'd never seen her wear this type of shoe. She told me she kept them for weddings, shaking her head and giving me a look as if to say I asked a lot of questions. I always did. But, throughout the rest of my childhood, at least I had one spiked pair of shoes to clomp around in while spending weekends at her house, until I was old enough to choose my own shoes.

Wearing my mother's shoes continued to be my passion as I grew up. Gratefully, at age thirteen, my feet stopped growing and caught up to my mother's perfect sample-size six and a half, enabling me to walk into any shoe store and try on shoes that were on display, without having to ask a salesperson to check my size. All my shoe dreams had come true. I wore my mother's shoes plenty throughout junior and high school years (most of the time she never knew). The shoe gods were kind to me.

As the decades passed, styles had changed, my preferences changed, and my museum of shoes continued to grow. When I hit my fifties and some heel-height sense kicked in, I slowly phased out the four-inchers and beyond. Nowadays three-inch heels are my cap; but then, there are always a few exceptions—a must-have pair of shoes I cannot resist, with a maximum allowable three-and-a-half-inch heel to be worn for minimal amounts of time. Arches and insoles make my feet happier, and summer Fitflops are my go-to now. But you'll still never catch me getting dolled up for an outing without my heels!

First Blood

May circa 1971, one month before my twelfth birthday, I dashed to my junior high school girls' bathroom. It was my first year, grade seven. I felt somewhat under the weather, and a cramping sensation made me think I'd wet my pants. With thighs squeezed tight, I scurried to the washroom to investigate what was going on down under. I pulled down my tight Wrangler jeans and plopped myself onto the toilet. And then I saw it. A small crimson pool had saturated my once-white underwear, and my thighs were stained red. *Holy shit*! I cried out. "What the hell is wrong with me?"

My mind raced as I tried to assess what on earth was happening to me. I went through a checklist of plausible reasons for the mini bloodbath between my legs but couldn't think of what I might have done to cause it. I knew I hadn't banged into anything, and I wasn't in dire pain. All I felt was a slight stretching of my innards. And no, I'd never even heard the word *menstruation*. What I feared most was, would the hemorrhaging ever stop? One thing I knew for certain—I wasn't about to tell a soul.

I cleaned up as best I could with what I had to work with, padded my underpants with approximately four inches thick of scruffy brown paper towels from the school bathroom dispensing machine and stole a bunch more to stash in my purse because I didn't know if that was the end of the affair or if there was more to come. If I'd had any education about what the horrifying event meant, I might have inserted a nickel into the sanitary pad dispenser—if I'd even known what they were for.

I was grateful the weather wasn't yet too warm, and I'd been wearing my Adidas hoodie at school that day. It came in handy to tie around my waist and cover the red stain on the back of my jeans. I remained in school for the rest of the day, then ran the almost two-mile distance home, eager to hop into the shower.

I removed my clothes and piled them neatly in a corner so I could throw them in the washer after my shower, no one else knowing the better. The makeshift padding of stacked paper towels had grown into a soggy scarlet mess. It appeared that perhaps this *bad thing* wasn't going away. The crimson tide carried on for another six days. I was mighty grateful school had not yet ended, because I relied heavily (pun intended) on those scratchy paper towels to get me through whatever was going on in my nether parts.

When at home, I used our household paper towels. At least they were softer! I kept my resolve never to tell a soul. I worried I'd either get in trouble because I'd done something bad or that something was wrong with me; and I didn't want to know. This event occurred three more times before I got caught.

You may wonder by now why I didn't scoop any sanitary napkins from my mother's stash. But I'd yet to learn what was happening to me and what tools were available to contain my new monthly floods. I had never seen a sanitary pad! That's how sheltered and uninformed I was. Besides my lack of information, I wouldn't have found anything helpful in mother's stash, since she'd had a complete hysterectomy at age twenty-nine. The words Kotex and tampon had never crossed my ears. Presumably, my mother never even considered keeping anything around for her eldest daughter. For her, it was out of sight, out of mind. There was no need for such items, as she had no use for them.

The thought of approaching my mother to inquire about the ongoing bloodbaths terrified me. I feared she'd scream at me for not telling her when my scarlet nightmares began. That was the sad truth. I never felt comfortable talking to my mother about personal issues, thoughts, or dreams. And I was thoroughly green about knowing anything related to the cliched *birds and bees*. My ignorance and discomfort about broaching personal issues held me back from asking about the red sea that formed between my legs. But in my mother's defense, I was only eleven years old, so she probably thought she still had a few years till she'd have to have that embarrassing talk with me. Maybe? So, there was no immediate need to leave a lousy box of Kotex pads lying around to prepare for the eventual day that came early. But hey, there were signs. After all, I was wearing a bra at age nine, so a little preparation on my mother's part would have been appreciated.

My mother was far from your average mamma. And never could I even try to picture her sitting me down and talking to me about the womanly woes. Eventually, I got caught *red-panted* while our family was on summer vacation at Fort Erie, Ontario, where we spent most of our childhood summer holidays with various family members and friends of my mother's. We had our babysitter from home staying with us afternoons at the motel, pool while Mother and friends would go to the racetrack. Yes, our family summer get-together destination was conveniently—in the same town where they ran the summer meet for the pony races. But I digress.

One summer evening, we were having dinner in the motel's attached restaurant when I felt the now familiar *trickle* between my legs. My heart almost stopped as, once again, I'd forgotten about that mysterious visitor who seemed to come and go. And more horrifying was the fact that I was wearing white pants! I jumped out of my chair, ran to the bathroom, and, unsurprisingly, my mother and aunt were hot on my trail. They caught me, literally, red-panted when they busted into the bathroom behind me. I can still envision my aunt trying to calm my dramatic mother. Aunty Sherry seemed cheery and congratulatory (although I didn't feel like this event was anything worthy of being congratulated for; more like humiliated) complimenting my mother about how her daughter just became a woman. My mother, however, exhibiting a scowled face, grilled me.

"Do you know what that blood is on your pants?" Her authoritative tone told me she knew exactly what had happened.

"No," I snarked. "Do you?"

"You're going to get this every month for a few days from now on," she snapped.

Despite what felt like a directive with no further explaining, I was relieved and psyched there'd be no punishment for what seemed an evil edict. She didn't ask if I'd ever had this happen before, and I surely wasn't volunteering it. In her next breath, she informed me that after we finish dinner, she'd ask Dad to drive us to the pharmacy to purchase some sanitary pads. I cringed.

"Mom, pleaseeeeee don't tell Daddy."

It was humiliating enough talking about this new and uncomfortable situation with my mother, let alone sharing this intimate information with my father. The thought of my father ever knowing anything of my personal *womanly* issues was mortifying. How could I face my father after that?

My mother promised she wouldn't tell him and said she'd take me to the pharmacy. But she lied.

Twenty minutes later, I was riding in the car with both my parents. The pharmacy was a little off the beaten path, and my father looked perturbed. He turned to my mother and asked her why the pharmacy couldn't wait until tomorrow when there was daylight. In the next horrific moment, my mother replied, "We have to get sanitary napkins for Debby tonight!"

The color of my face undoubtedly became the same shade as the stain on my pants. My biggest humiliation in life had just happened. My blabbermouth mother let my father know that I'd become a woman that day. I didn't have the nerve to divulge my earlier bleeds to my mother because of embarrassment, so letting my father know was the ultimate humiliation. Little did I know that would be the first of many betrayals by my mother. But the best part was I no longer had to suffer diaper rash from those scratchy brown paper towels, I was well-stocked at home, and I was relieved to learn I didn't have some scary life-threatening disease that I would eventually bleed to death from.

My First Kiss— Yuck!

I was naive to both love and relationships. I knew nothing about sex, love, or even about kissing. I was nine years old and about to get an education.

My dad and grandfather ran a family business. They had a huge plant, a wholesale fish company near downtown Toronto. The building was located on a street corner where, serendipitously, the annual Santa Claus parade passed right by the building each November. Every year the parade would fill the wintry streets with people standing huddled together to keep warm as they watched the parade pass by. I was fortunate not to freeze and enjoy the parade in warmth, as the front offices of Dad's building faced directly to the street. The employees were invited to bring their children to work, to enjoy the parade. There were always plenty of doughnuts and chocolate milk as treats to indulge in as we basked in the warmth and comfort of the office and watched the parade.

Tim was my father's top salesman, and he'd bring his son Bobby every year to watch the parade. Bobby and I became friends. By the time I was nine years old, my parents had grown close with Bobby's parents, and sometimes they'd come over to spend a Sunday afternoon at our house. I'd experience a butterfly sensation inside me whenever Bobby and I were alone together.

One day, Bobby and I were in the basement playing *house* of all things. I was the mother, and he was the father. Bobby caught me quite off-guard when he leaned in and planted a big wet kiss on me. And it was no regular kiss. He stuck his tongue in my mouth. Yuck! Despite my finding that kiss disgusting, I didn't pull away. But all the while my head was swarming with questions. *What on earth is this weird style of kissing? Does this make me a bad girl? Am I going to get germs? Why were our tongues mingling together? What is happening here?* Gross!

When I finally pulled away, feeling confused but somehow warm and fuzzy, I asked Bobby why he stuck his tongue down my throat. How naïve was I? He informed me that's how people kiss when they *really* like each other. I learned something new.

Apparently, according to Bobby, that kiss meant I was now officially his girlfriend. *So that's how relationships happen*, I thought.

Bobby's family didn't live near us, and our visits were limited to whenever our parents would get together—and once a year at the parade. I didn't feel as though I was wildly pining for him in between our visits, but when we did get together, the butterflies danced within, and I learned to like the kissing bit. Our on-and-off part-time relationship continued for another two years. By the time we were to enter junior high school at our respective schools, we were making new friends, and our desires led us in different directions.

Although nothing further developed between us, we remained friends for years to come. And I never forgot that Bobby was *the one* who taught me how to kiss.

First Broken Heart

B arry lived across the street from us when we lived in our big white house. The newly developed neighborhood had only two houses built at first—ours and Barry's. Playing outside was a favorite pastime. Riding bikes and outdoor games kept us kids busy after school till the first streetlight shone its beams into the darkness, like a school bell alerting playtime was over and we must go inside.

Barry's family moved in halfway through the school year, so he would finish the year at his old school before joining my junior high after the summer. I was twelve, Barry was eleven. We became good friends, and our friendship quickly blossomed into romance.

Barry's kisses were not my first kisses, but Barry was my first love. We spent most of our time together after school and on weekends, going for walks, holding hands, and kissing. Many evenings we'd sit outside together on a street curb and look at the stars, sharing dreams and aspirations, planning our future together at the ripe old ages of twelve and eleven, and talking about eloping. What the heck did we even know about eloping? We'd both come from broken homes, and the convenience of *boy meets girl* living on the same street was probably half our attraction to each other.

But we were *madly* in love. His term of endearment for me was *Debby Delish*. My gawd, I still have the love letters he sent me from camp that summer . . . when he left me behind. Literally.

During June and July, we did many things together, from outside activities to watching movies and stealing *intimate* time together when our parents weren't around. Of course, there were limits. Not to say Barry didn't try breaking limits, but the fear of my mother ever finding out I even kissed a boy was strong enough to keep my hormones in check.

We had what some would call a fantasy puppy-love relationship. We had much in common—broken homes, siding with our fathers, and mothers who were barely ever at home. Who knows if these common threads contributed to our attraction. Whatever the reasons, our relationship filled a void for one another. When we weren't together, we'd chat on the phone for hours. My bedroom window faced his and was kitty-corner. After our evening chats ended, we'd flick our bedroom lights using the code we'd invented—translation—I love you. We also used the flickering lights to get each other's attention, so my bedroom window became somewhat of a lookout post. We enjoyed spending most of our time together whenever we had the opportunity. But things were about to change.

Barry got a job at sleepover camp as a junior counselor for the month of August. I missed him and mourned the loss of companionship before he even left, just thinking about enduring loneliness in his absence. There was no shortage of love letters sent back-and-forth between us. My heart pumped endorphins daily as I awaited the mailman. It was the blue envelope I kept my eye out for. Every one of those letters began: Dear Delish. The days grew so long for me as I awaited Barry's arrival home, despite our family vacation to Fort Erie during most of August.

The anticipation of Barry's return surged within me. I dreamed of when he'd once again hold me, making me feel as though he was the only person in the world who really knew and loved me. But worry eclipsed my anticipation when, by the last week or so of August, I never received another letter from him.

A common occurrence in the world of puppy-love (just as in the world of grown-up love) is, when lovers separate for some time, shit can happen.

I counted the days and hours till Barry would return. Finally, the day came. Peeking out from my bedroom window, the anticipation was intense while waiting for the big yellow bus to bring him home. Then there he was! When he grabbed his duffle bag and made his way up his driveway, I darted down our spiral staircase and bolted out the front door to greet him. I called out to him as he approached his front door, expecting him to drop everything and run to me, like they did in the movies. But Barry shouted back that he had to put his stuff away and would come outside soon. In that moment, I knew.

I knew something was up when Barry didn't reciprocate the same familiar urgency. I suspected a problem when he stopped sending love letters. And now, after almost a month's separation, he had no desire to take me in his arms and hug me like in all the movies I'd watched.

Barry never came back outside that day, nor did he call me. It was already dusk and there were no flickering lights in response to my bedroom light distress signals. There was no way I was going to sleep that night without speaking with him. Despite the darkness, I went over to his house and knocked on the door. Barry answered. I instantly could see his eyes no longer held the passion they once showed me, and he gave me a half-hearted hug— the kind you might give an acquaintance or as a polite greeting. He then informed me he was no longer my boyfriend.

In an instant I felt my heart shatter into a million pieces. In that same instant I had to swallow the fact that, only a few months prior, the guy who declared he was crazy in love with me and wanted us to elope and spend our life together, the guy I pined over the whole time he was away, had just informed me he was sorry but already had a new girlfriend he'd met at camp—Linda.

I knew Linda from my first year in junior high. She had massive boobs and was in with the *mean girl* crowd. In fact, she was the ringleader. Maybe I'm being petty, but she wasn't even pretty. At that age, however, boobs trumped everything else important to a relationship, and she was more than well-endowed.

I sobbed broken-hearted tears for days, mostly secluded in my room until school began, hoping Barry would realize how much he missed me and come running back to me—like often happened in the movies.

I didn't know Linda-with-the-boobs well, but I'd seen her in action being mean to people while strutting down the school halls like her shit didn't stink. And I never expected to become her next victim to taunt and bully. It became clear that if she didn't know me before, she definitely knew me now. She loved to bang into me in the hallways and rub in my face how much better she was, reminding me this was why her now boyfriend left me. I was already a nervous child, but now I carried a broken heart and was bullied by my ex-boyfriend's new girlfriend. Who was the jealous one?

One day while in the girls' bathroom at school, I overheard gossip about Linda gathering her posse of mean girls and preparing to wait for me outside after school so they could beat me up. According to what I heard, they wanted to *beat the shit out of me.* Me—the one who got dumped was now going to get beat up by the hussy who stole my boyfriend. I jetted out of the bathroom and went straight to the principal's office to let them know what I'd overheard and ask if I could call my mother to ask her to pick me up after school.

I waited in the school lobby, anxiously looking through the glass while my eyes focused on the nasty mean girls gathered just outside the doors. Grateful when my mother pulled up in her blue

Buick Skylark, I called out and dashed toward her. As she stepped out of the car, I watched the evil clique disperse and make like there were no ill intentions planned. My mother told me she'd already spoken with the principal to ensure these shenanigans would end.

$\sim\!\!\!\sim\quad\sim\!\!\!\sim$

Years later, I ran into a friend of Barry's while at some high school get-together. We laughed about our junior high school days. Then he shared with me that long after junior high ended, Barry commented to him he let the *right one* get away. Turns out, boobs weren't enough to cement a relationship.

My First Driving Lesson – Oye!

I was a curious child. Growing up with an inquisitive mind always came with apprehension. I began my journey of growing up as a worrywart at a young age. I'm not sure if that worry stemmed from my responsibilities and fear of failure, of having to succeed at new things that were integral parts of growing up, or if I was just an over-thinker about everything. Questions most children asked naturally as their awareness and curiosity grew were difficult for me, because I lacked confidence in asking questions.

I worried about things I'm sure most children don't usually give a second thought. I was probably age eight when I first became fascinated by the thermostat in our home. How on earth did that thing work? How would I ever know what those buttons were for? How can that little box on the dining room wall possibly control making a house warm or cool by simply moving a dial? But I never asked. Before my thermostat worries, my first concern was wondering how I'd ever learn to tie my shoelaces. How would I ever learn these simple yet, complex things?

The same question plagued me about the possibility of one day learning to drive a car. The closest I'd ever come to knowing anything about driving a car was when my father put me on his lap while driving to the variety store, a mere few blocks away from our home, and allowed me to hold the steering wheel. I was totally unaware he was driving because I didn't see his hands holding the bottom of the steering wheel. Sure, Dad was driving, but it sure felt as if I were large and in charge of his big black Buick Wildcat.

Those were fun times for me, feeling like a big girl. But as I grew into a young teen, the thought of handling a beastly machine, like a car, became exciting, as I was sure driving was the least of my worries to master. After all, I rode as a passenger in a car with my dad a zillion times, and it looked so effortless—insert key, start engine, put the gear in drive.

By the time I turned sixteen, I was more than ready to learn how to drive and gain my wings of freedom. I dreamed of the freedom to go anywhere without the mile walk to the bus stop and the subsequent several buses required to get to anywhere, including school, especially in the elements.

I didn't hesitate to get started. On my sixteenth birthday I acquired what was known back then as my 365 learners permit. The permit enabled me to drive with a licensed driver in the car. It was the steppingstone to gaining a full driver's license so I could eventually drive anywhere on my own.

At first Dad said he'd take me out a few times to teach me how to drive, adding he was sure I'd catch on quickly. But the only thing that happened was his change of mind. Dad took me out for a lesson the next day after receiving my 365. It was the mid-late 1970s, and even mid-sized cars were as big as boats. So, one could well-imagine that Dad's huge silver Sedan Deville Cadillac was even longer than the average mid-sized car. But I wasn't at all intimidated by its size, because cars in our family were always large.

Dad started the engine, then stepped out of the car and moved to the passenger seat so I could take command of the wheel. I was clueless about all the components of a car. I knew zippo about car mechanics and felt overwhelmed by all the functions and gizmos, but my father went over everything thoroughly. Some stuck in my head, and some would require a refresher course. And then it was time to put the car in drive.

I was grateful my dad had parked the car on the circular part of our driveway and not the long part in front of the double garage, so I didn't have to drive in reverse. With my foot on the brake, as instructed, I pulled the gearshift into drive and then moved my foot from the brake to the gas . . . with a little too much gas. "Hit the brake!" Dad shouted. And did I ever. The big heavy beast jerked to a stop. We'd yet to leave the driveway, and I could already sense my father was apprehensive about taking his eldest child out for her first driving lesson. Our house was on a corner, so all I had to do was turn left out of the drive and then a quick right at the stop sign, taking us onto a side street that led to the main road. But there would be no main road driving for me that day.

I pulled out of the driveway keeping my foot on the brake, with a few intermittent fast hard brakes, sprinkled with a few heavy goes at the gas pedal before approaching that first stop sign.

After Dad assisted me with that *first turn*, I did what I'd seen people do a thousand times in the movies: I steered that wheel up and down and side-to-side. Luckily it was the side street and not the main road. But Dad put a stop to the insanity. He taught me to relax with the steering wheel and not move it around randomly, to focus on the road ahead and the parked cars on the street, and to stay away from the parked cars. My whiplash-like driving method was scaring the crap out of my father. My adrenalin was pumping with excitement and concern about just how I was going to dodge the parked cars on the right. I'd yet to develop a sense of judgment about how close I was or was not to those parked cars, so naturally I wanted to keep as far from that side of the street as possible . . . until I saw the oncoming car and I panicked. How on earth would there be enough room for the parked cars on the side, the oncoming car on the left, and me in the middle? Dad knew instinctively, in that split-second, that I was petrified about the parked cars and wavering about the oncoming one.

In a flash, my dad grabbed the wheel and navigated around and in-between the parked cars and the oncoming one. As soon as we approached some vacant curbside space, Dad had me put my foot on the brake while he reached over and put the car in park. He got out of the car and told me to get in the passenger seat. Dad was driving us home after a mere couple of blocks of my driving. He announced he couldn't take the pressure and would sign me up for private driving instruction.

I must give my father credit for wanting even to attempt teaching his daughter to drive. He was so nervous, but he wanted to do what every good father did for their kids . . . he just couldn't follow through. But the fiasco didn't intimidate me, and I was rather proud of myself for acquiring this new-found power that would become the vehicle to my personal freedom.

Once I finally got my official driver's license, I felt free as a lark. My mother, picked up daily by her friends for busy social-life jaunts and thus hardly ever at home, gave me almost full-time use of her big white Cadillac Coupe. I no longer had to suffer the mile walks to the bus stop and the three buses to my high school. No more taking three buses to the shopping mall or having to beg for a ride to visit a friend. Chauffeur duties came along with driving privileges. I really didn't mind because I truly loved the freedom I felt as a driver, and the novelty of having a vehicle to transport me anywhere I wanted to go was so worth the privilege.

My First Car Accident—Sort of

I'd had only had my driver's license for a few months, and already had become a good driver. No doubt the access I had to my mother's car gave me good experience. It kept me busy driving to school and back daily, running errands as a personal chauffeur, and, of course, fulfilling my passion for retail therapy every Saturday—all of which beat taking a bus by a longshot. There were still days when my mother required her car, leaving the memories of taking the bus never far away. But the best times were when Dad went on vacation, because he always left me his car for my personal use—except for the first time, just a few months after receiving my license. I only had the car for two days of the glorious two weeks I was to have it at my disposal.

I'll preface this little incident by saying that my paternal grandfather didn't share the same enthusiasm for my having access to my father's Cadillac. My grandfather's views on the modern life of a woman's place, and a sixteen-year-old girl driving around in her father's Cadillac, clashed with mine. The man was old-school with ancient views, and we locked horns in most of our conversations. He was from the school of thought where boys were more important than girls. Grandsons held favor, and he made no bones about concealing that. When I'd question him about his prejudices and dark age beliefs, he thought I was some wild child who knew too much for her own good, never failing to remind me. There was no great love lost between us, or if there were, I wasn't privy to it. But out of respect for my father, my siblings and I maintained the family tradition of visiting my grandparents' home for the traditional Sabbath dinner for as long as they lived. I resented having to go there, but I went.

I pulled up to the patriarchal home on Friday evening. Dad had left two days prior for Miami. The home was a ranch style bungalow on a corner lot. Several eighteen-inch metal posts were linked by chains spread along the property where the grass met the curb at the front of the house. The driveway was at the backside of the house, so just as Dad always did, I parked in front of the house along the curb. I kept the visit short—eat dinner, have some meaningless conversation, and I was out of there, eager to get home and get ready to go out with my friends.

I said my goodbyes and hopped into the car, relieved to be going and not having to endure hearing repetitive lectures from my grandfather about how much my father spoiled me, adding that a young girl should not be driving around in her father's Cadillac.

My grandfather made me nervous and uncomfortable, and even more so by standing on the front porch, and watching me drive off. I turned the key in the ignition, started the engine, then reversed a bit to gather some room so I could drive out around the vehicle that had parked too close in front of me. Once I put the car back in drive to make my exit, it wouldn't move. I double-checked to make sure the gear was in drive and then pushed hard on the gas pedal, but to no avail. The engine just roared. And through the side mirror, I saw my grandfather amble his way to the car looking dismayed and waving his hands in the air to signal me to stop. I put the car in park and stepped out to the familiar sound of the only swear word I'd ever heard my grandfather use. "Goddammit, look what you've done. I told your father not to leave you the goddamn keys." Ignoring his rant, I looked behind the car to check what was going on.

Somehow, when I reversed the car, the undercarriage hinged over one of the metal poles lining the curb, holding the car hostage. I was mortified. And I retorted, "Look what happened after you made me so nervous by reprimanding me because my father lent me his car." I was convinced my grandfather had either wished the incident on me or had made his emphatic views loud and clear to the universe, bringing on the incident. Then he demanded I hand over the keys and informed me I wouldn't be getting them back. He then proceeded back to the house to get his own car keys so he could drive me home while nattering on about how he'd have to call a tow truck when he returned, to lift the car off the pole. My resentment toward him brewed as we remained silent all the way home. And at the same time, I worried about what he'd tell my dad.

I was not afraid of my father. I just felt bad for potentially damaging his car. My grandfather told me he would have the car repaired and wouldn't tell my father about it until his return. I wasn't about to wait two weeks embroiled in angst. I called Dad the next day and informed him about the entire incident. Dad blurted out his favorite word, a resounding *shit*, and then let me know it was no big deal. He told me the car would be repaired, nobody was hurt, and gave me permission to skip having to go back to my grandparents' home until he returned. I loved my dad.

My First Car

I was fortunate to have had lots of access to a vehicle when I was a teen, both my mother's and father's cars. A few months after my sixteenth birthday, at my mother's insistence, my father moved away from home for the last time. It was the inevitable and long overdue final breakup of my parents' marriage—a whole other book. Two-and-a-half years later, when I moved away from my dysfunctional family home, my life began.

My new apartment was in midtown of my city, closer to downtown than the more northerly burbs where I was raised. There was a bus stop right outside my building, and the subway was a mere ten-minute walk. Many of my friends had cars, and my part-time job was conveniently located inside the building where I lived. I worked as a receptionist a few days a week and on Saturdays in the recreation center. The odd time I needed a car, I'd borrow my father's. His business was only a fifteen-minute drive from my place. One of Dad's employees would pick me up, drive me back to the business, and Dad would lend me his car till the end of the workday, when he'd drive me home. Then, as became protocol, Dad would take us out for dinner to our favorite Chinese restaurant near where I lived, then drop me back at home. I loved our Daddy-daughter time together. When Dad went on vacation, I had his car full-time—except for that one time when I'd hitched the back of his car to a pole. Then one day, my father surprised me with my very own car, two months before my twenty-first birthday.

Saturdays were fun days to work, as all the regular members would come in on weekends for a swim or workout, and I'd become friends with many of them. Many would make a pit stop in my office for a visit and conversation. Work was like a social event there. Who would show up was always a surprise. My father often popped by on the odd Saturday to visit and have a catch up in my compact office. There wasn't much work to do on weekends, aside from answering the phones and keeping an eye out in the center to make sure nobody wore street shoes in the gym. But one Saturday in April, my dad came 'round unexpectedly and brought one of my brother's friends, who worked part-time for him.

I rose from my chair and walked around the desk to hug Dad, surprised he'd brought company with him. I was delighted to see them and jokingly asked what they were up to. Dad had a huge grin on his face as he reached into his pant pocket, pulled out a set of car keys, and placed them on my desk. With beaming pride on his face, he exclaimed, "Happy Birthday!"

I was the most surprised I'd ever been. I had no clue my father was buying me a car and couldn't believe he pulled one over one me. I remembered back to the time when I was sixteen and received my driver's license. My father was so proud of me and told me he was going to buy me a car. But that idea was short-lived when my mother ranted on about how foolish it was for a sixteen-year-old to have her own car. End of story, nothing to discuss, never mentioned again, until my wonderful surprise car came to fruition.

I hugged my father again for giving me the beautiful gift of independence. The excitement had me locking up the office and placing the phone lines on hold, so I could check out my new wheels of freedom. My eyes beheld a most wondrous sight, for there parked on the side street was my shiny, brand new, white Ford Mustang. My Dad beamed with pride as he stood by the curb watching me take it for a test drive around the block. I came back, jumped out, and gave him another huge hug. Then he and my brother's friend left together in Dad's car.

My First Big European Vacation

I never asked for the trip. It was my eighteenth birthday gift from my father. Dad decided it would be beneficial for me to see a bit of the world. He booked me a six-week student trip to Europe and Israel, with a tour group from ages eighteen to twenty-two. I'd go in the summer—a mere eight months before I moved away from home. This adventure offered an eye-opening experience of different cultures and a chance to see how other parts of the world lived.

There were sixteen of us young adults from Toronto and New York. I flew to New York to meet up with the group and the thirty-year-old tour guide named Miriam. Shortly after meeting up, we all set off to London, England. After London we'd travel to Israel for three weeks, and then on to France, Italy, and Switzerland; possibly not in that order, but it was a long time ago. During one of those three weeks in Israel, we'd stay on a kibbutz. A kibbutz is a collective community settlement where citizens (and visitors) live on the same vast piece of land leased to the community by the state. Everyone earns their keep by contributing and having a designated job within the community. Visitors pay to stay in the kibbutz hotel, where the rooms are more like dorms. Guests must contribute and are given a daily job on the land. I have a plethora of memories from that trip, too many for this book, but certainly, some are too poignant and hilarious not to share.

I was at my heaviest weight ever. Almost a year had passed since I'd been on that last crazy keto-like diet of barely eating anything substantial for months, turning almost anorexic-looking, now on a complete 180, gaining the weight all back, plus. I was immensely insecure about my looks and weight, despite the compliments telling me I was pretty and starting to look like my mother. However, I'm not sure if it was self-shame or vanity that prompted ideas about how best to camouflage my not-so-finer parts. Packing for that trip consisted of a few skirts and tops, many high-heeled shoes, ONE dreaded bathing suit, pajamas, underwear, and a carry-on full of cosmetics and beauty products. I felt all I had going for me was my face and a sense of humor, so I focused my attention on making myself as presentable as best I could.

My high heels were my imagined *thinning aid*. I'd learned from reading fashion magazines that taller equaled thinner-looking. I was eager and opened to anything that would help to disguise the heft I carried on my size sixteen body, which not so long before was close to a size four. Oh, sure they sent me a packing list before-hand, but shorts, bathing suits (plural), and sneakers were definitely not occupying my suitcase. So, I traveled and toured everywhere, from museums to galleries to ruins, in my four-inch high heels. I kid you not.

Meeting people and becoming fast-friends has always come naturally to me. While on the plane from Toronto to New York, I befriended two guys from the tour who traveled together, Harvey, and Huey. They were four years my senior and loved to laugh. So did I. It wasn't long before we were dubbed The Three Musketeers by tour-guide Miriam, who seemed threatened by me and my effervescent per-sonality. There were no romantic interludes with the guys. It was purely platonic, almost as though I had two big brothers looking out for me. I seemed to gather more male friends than female on that trip. The girls were rather snotty, and save for two of them, I didn't forge any other relationships of significance. I felt some girls shied away from me because my outlandish dress code or my jovial and large personality intimidated them. Harvey and Huey saw past my outside appearance. They laughed with me and not at me. Those two guys were a godsend. They kept an eye out for me. When we toured and they saw me struggle to climb rocks and ruins with my four-inch spikes, they were at my side, each grabbing an arm to help me through the rubble. And we'd collectively burst out laughing as they reprimanded me for not wearing flats or sneakers.

We spent three weeks touring Israel, covering much of the country with daily bus tours to different cities and historical sites. Joseph was our designated bus driver throughout our time in Israel. He was a cheery, short, burly man who loaded and unloaded our luggage at every rest stop, ate with us, and laughed with us. Whenever I'd look straight ahead while on that bus, I'd catch him staring at me through his rear-view mirror. I knew nothing about the man as he couldn't speak a word of English, yet I was flattered that he cast his sights on me and came to my rescue at every opportunity—until one day while walking through some ruins—he planted a kiss on me.

Butterflies hummed within as I felt somewhat special knowing a man was attracted to me, despite knowing nothing about him, and even though he was nearly two decades older than me. Regardless of the language barrier, Joseph took great strides to communicate with me. I knew only a few Hebrew words, which is a completely different language than the old European Yiddish I was more familiar with from my paternal grandparents. Joseph would often repeat a phrase to me, a phrase I didn't understand. So I repeated it to Harvey, who spoke Hebrew, because my curiosity got the best of me. Harvey busted a gut laughing after I spoke the phrase to him. He told me the phrase translated as "I love you and I want to kiss you." Oye! I certainly didn't sign up for any distorted love affair stuff, so it was almost perfect timing that our last destination in Israel was spending a week on a kibbutz working the land to earn our keep, then we'd be off to another country. I was no farm girl, coming from a big city, so I was almost grateful they assigned me the job of picking weeds daily, and even more grateful the kibbutz stay was the end of the line for our bus driver Joseph.

Kibbutz life was just not for me. I complained daily to Miriam like a spoiled brat. "I didn't sign up for this. I'm supposed to be on holiday, not picking weeds daily at 5:00 a.m." Oh yes, I sounded like a spoiled child, mostly because I was, and it was my first time traveling alone.

Miriam looked more male than female. At eighteen, my intuition was already sharp. I knew Miriam was getting fed up with The Three Musketeers, tired of our continual laughter, and probably tired of my complaining. Perhaps she felt threatened by my bold personality. I was the bubbly girl who'd talk to everyone and anyone, spreading laughter despite language barriers and causing a few shenanigans wherever I went. I felt Miriam just craved being included. She seemed lonely. And despite my extra weight and flamboyant style of dressing, I couldn't help but feel she was envious of my outgoing personality and my ability to socialize and mingle. I didn't give it a lot of thought back then, but hindsight always gives us better vision. There were a few very attractive girls on our tour, complete with great bodies, yet Miriam's focus was on me. Even though she knocked on my hotel room door at times and ask me to teach her how to apply make-up, and despite my good nature and favors I did for her, she still pulled a few tricks on me before our truce came to be.

Shenanigans. Let's just say that awakening at 4:30 a.m. to get ready for kibbutz duty wasn't appealing to me. Outside work began at 5:00 a.m. to prevent working late into the day under the hot Mediterranean sun. By the third day, I rebelled and decided not to show up for weed-picking duty until around 7:00 a.m., when we'd receive first break and breakfast. I didn't think I'd be missed, but the clock foiled my good intentions. Just after 7:00 a.m., when everyone should have been communing for breakfast, I heard what sounded like a cackle of laughing hyenas enter my dorm.

The sound of loud voices and laughter filled my room. Before I realized I wasn't dreaming, a bucket of water was poured on my head. Harvey and Huey and a few others from the group were standing over my bed, howling with laughter as I leapt out of bed, startled almost to death and soaking wet. Apparently, the group didn't feel it was fair that I was lounging in bed while they tended to chores at an ungodly hour. I joined in the laughter, knowing I most certainly deserved their cruel prank.

It was a different time and a different world in the mid-1970s. I knew nothing about politics or war and certainly didn't know the laws of each country I visited. Perhaps it was my gift of gab that obscured my ability to listen, as I may have missed some important rules when announced.

One Friday night in Jerusalem, our group went to visit the Wailing Wall. I was excited to see with my own eyes what I'd learned about that holy place, the last remaining western wall of the Second

Temple of Jerusalem, a place of prayer and pilgrimage destroyed by the Romans (70 ce).

Men and women stood in the vast open area with prayer books in hand, prayer shawls draped around their shoulders, chanting aloud Torah passages and prayers to God. I was an observer, save for the ritual of writing a wish on a small piece of paper, folding it up tiny, and placing it among the thousands of notes in a crack in the wall to leave a prayer behind.

With the huge Sabbath crowd coveting their prized standing spots in front of the Wall, I was determined to take some photos of the infamous site. I scouted out a quiet spot on a raised hill further back from the crowd with a good vantage point. I'd invited Harvey to stand back there with me to take some photos. There we stood like proud tourists, our trusted cameras with blinding flashbulbs clicking away, when a soldier in full camo attire approached, his big-ass rifle pointing at me. In broken best-attempt-to-speak-in English and Hebrew combined, he informed us that taking photos on the Sabbath was forbidden. Apparently, we missed reading the sign; and, by all rights, we should have known better. Orthodox Judaism doesn't allow using electronic devices on the Sabbath. I will blame my nonsensical thinking that on vacation, rules don't apply.

After the soldier reprimanded us, he told us to wait exactly where we were standing and said he'd be right back. I may not have known much about war or politics, but I knew enough . . . a soldier with a big gun just informed me I broke a law in a strange country. I wasn't about to wait around for something scary to go down.

Harvey and I locked eyes and understood through telepathy that we'd better run for our lives. And we did! I can't remember how far or for how long we ran—past the Wall, through the Arab market, and finally reaching a city street where we grabbed the first cab we saw. I never even bothered to find out what the punishment was for breaking that law on the Sabbath, and I never visited the Wall again. I felt as though I may have been on some wanted list. And that incident became a comical story between Harvey and me. We'd remind one another randomly throughout the rest of the tour. It made us remember how delicious our freedom tasted.

We were now in Tiberias by the Sea of Galilee, about thirty kilometers from Nazareth, staying in dorm-like rooms, separate from the main hotel building, about a ten-minute walk to the main building's dining room. Admittedly, I was a young rebellious teen and felt justified in my convictions that if I was on vacation, I didn't have to take part in events that weren't appealing to me.

We'd been touring out in the 130-degree desert heat all day. Sweating and exhausted, we returned to the hotel in late afternoon, a welcome respite from the blazing, searing sun. We had a few hours of personal time to swim, rest, and freshen up for a special dinner out that evening at a restaurant in town. The bus was to pick us up at 6:30 p.m. I took advantage of the spare time to sneak in a quick nap, but when I awoke, it was pitch dark and my roommate was nowhere in sight. I didn't yet have a watch (my plan was to buy one in Switzerland), and bewildered, I wondered, *where is everyone*? Panic arose within. I didn't know what scared me more—staying alone in a secluded building in pitch of darkness or braving the trek to the main building dining hall with no outside lights to guide. But I was hungry and clueless about what time it was, so I put on my big girl pants and dashed, as quickly as my stilettos would permit, over to the main building.

All was quiet. The grand heavy doors leading to the dining hall were locked. I ran inside the main lobby, elated to find someone behind the desk, and asked what time it was. It was 10:30 p.m.! I surely must have been zonked sleeping for so long that Miriam and the gang left me behind! Nobody even attempted to wake me—not even my two best amigos. It was payback for my whining and complaining, no doubt. There would be no dinner for me that night, as I sat outside the lobby for another hour waiting for the bus to pull up with the group. I had zero intentions of walking back to the dorm alone.

The bus returned, and many from the group chuckled when they saw me sitting alone on a bench. Some were smug, thinking they pulled a good one on me once again. And my trusted amigos looked concerned fearing I was angry with them. But as soon as we locked eyes, we broke out laughing. To my dismay, however, there were no doggie bags!

I came, I saw, I awakened, and I had enough of Israel. I was eager to get to Rome.

Rome, the city of love, beautiful people, delicious food, and fabulous shopping! Ricardo, a cliché of the tall, dark, and handsome, was the bus driver who'd take us around Rome, Florence, and Pisa. We'd finally part enroute to Venice, say arrivederci, then hop on the water taxi to Venice.

Ricardo didn't speak a word of English, but the power of eye contact filled the gap between our language barriers. Ricardo drove us around daily. He'd stand proudly, in all his handsome demeanor, awaiting us to board the bus each morning. And his chivalrous efforts to assist the girls up the steps of the bus didn't go unnoticed.

There were two snooty girls in our group who were much more *princessly* than I ever was. But there must have been something about me and bus drivers, because chubby old me was the one who fetched their attention. Just as Joseph did in Israel, Ricardo kept his eye on me from the rear-view mirror. It didn't feel creepy as it might do in today's world, but rather flattering how I'd been the one to capture the eye of one very handsome bus driver who spoke no words of English.

Like Joseph in Israel, Ricardo loaded and unloaded our luggage at every hotel stop. As soon as he spotted me, he'd take my *extremely* overweight luggage right up to my room and he'd do the same for each hotel stop we made. This was a great help to me. Early mornings, high heels, and lugging a massive suitcase was a bit of a trod, so I welcomed Ricardo's help. On our third day of touring, he was waiting for me at lunch break time. As we piled off the bus, Ricardo invited me, using hand signals and his inviting smiling onyx-black eyes, to join him at a picnic table lunch. I accepted. By that time, I'd learned a few words in Italian, so we communicated in broken Ital-English conversation.

What did I know? I was young, curious, and impulsive. This very handsome man from a foreign country was interested in me. And this girl who was used to feeling insignificant, was flattered. So naturally, I eventually permitted him to kiss me. I was only eighteen and still living at home with the fear-of-God words from my mother about sex and how nice girls didn't do *those things*, implying I'd surely end up pregnant. Those were the warnings and usual scary threats my mother offered as her worldly and motherly advice. Nonetheless, the fear stuck with me, so there would be nothing more than butterfly kisses with Ricardo, despite my surmising that some of his communications meant understanding he undoubtedly wanted more.

By the sixth day, we were leaving Rome and off to Venice. Ricardo and I shared a few private moments to say goodbye after we'd finally arrived and got dropped at a water taxi station. I left him my address after he signaled to me that he'd like to stay in touch and write to me.

Upon my return, he wrote one letter per month for the next eight months. I left no forwarding address when I moved to my own apartment, so Ricardo had no way of keeping in touch. I never got to know Ricardo well enough. Besides our language barrier, time and circumstances held us back from digging deeper to learn more pertinent information about one another. I may have been a passing fancy for him, just another tourist, but for me, Ricardo was a good dose of beautiful for my pitiful lack of self-esteem. For a short time in my young loner life, I felt special and desired.

For all I know, Ricardo may well have been married. I didn't know and the thought never crossed my mind at the time, never anticipating anything more than a friendly flirtation with a stranger who just happened to be good for my soul at a vulnerable time in my life.

In later years when I'd reminisce about Ricardo the bus driver, I realized things I wasn't aware of back then: the return address on his letters belonged to the bus company where he worked; no home address. His letters were adoring and charming. I had one of my Italian girlfriends translate some of his letters. For Ricardo, I was some passing young foreign interlude. I wonder if he knew how much of a great boost he was to my once sorely lacking ego, making me feel significant.

I learned a lot about myself that summer.

My First Cigarette and How it Happened

I grew up in a smoke-filled home. Just about every adult I'd ever known was a smoker, and my parents were no exception. I think the only people I knew who didn't smoke were my paternal grandparents. They weren't smokers, yet always had ashtrays placed around side tables for guests.

The smell never bothered me, mostly because everywhere I went there were smokers. Back in the day, smoking was permitted everywhere—even on airplanes! The scent in my home was just part of home, a familiar smell I took for home. I was immune to the smell really, so I'd never thought about it.

My mother smoked much more than my father. She'd often leave a cigarette in an ashtray with a growing ember as it slowly burned to ash, as she'd proceed to light another. I had no opinion either way, because smoking was a part of social norms growing up in my era. When I think back to those days when people smoked everywhere, I find it astounding.

People smoked in lineups at the bank. Doctors smoked while consulting with us in their offices! People smoked on airplanes, using the built-in armrest ashtrays in their assigned smoking rows. I found it both scary and laughable. What the heck did smoking rows matter if you were the first row behind a smoking section, sucking back all the second-hand smoke? Oh right, nobody spoke of second-hand smoke back in the day. And what about if someone started a fire with their cigarette, accidentally of course, but still?

Smoke never bothered me. It still doesn't. And as much as it never bothered me, it also didn't appeal to me. But that doesn't mean I wasn't curious about what all the fun was about smoking. I had no clue that it was an addictive habit or what pleasure anyone got from it. But I was curious.

When I was eleven years old and my mother was out for the day, my curiosity piqued as I was tidying up the house. An ashtray containing a couple of half-smoked butts resting on a small pile of ashes intrigued me. I wasn't sure what came over me or why on that day or why I was so curious, but I was determined to find out what all the fuss was about.

I picked up a half-smoked cigarette butt, wiped it clean, grabbed a pack of matches off the kitchen counter, struck a match, lit the butt, and dragged on it— and just about coughed my head off. Yuck! The little coughing fit accompanied by dizziness had me almost falling into a kitchen chair. I remember sitting for a moment in amazement, wondering what the heck all the buzz was about this smoking business? I didn't understand what the big deal was. I wondered how anyone could enjoy the awful taste and dizzying feeling I experienced from only one drag, let alone smoking all day, every day. I had zero knowledge about the dangers of smoking. Why would I? I also didn't know that once people became smokers, the addictive components would keep them smoking. I never touched another cigarette until the last year of high school.

My friend Lori introduced me to the world of nightclubs just before finishing high school. Lori had already joined the club scene and introduced me to social smoking. My first cigarette was a Kool menthol, because that's what Lori smoked. She offered me one, and I told her I didn't smoke. Lori was a staunch smoker for a few years already. And it seemed the smoke-filled and low-lit nightclub atmosphere was a natural place for smoking, accompanied by an alcoholic beverage. The two went together nicely.

Lori flicked open her pack of Kools, and with a lighter in her other hand, eagerly informed me how well cigarettes and alcohol went together. She goaded me on, urging that I give smoking a try. "You want to look like you fit in." She coaxed me to just hold it splayed between my two fingers, light it, and if I didn't enjoy it, to just keep holding it and flicking ash until it burned down, so people would think I looked cool.

I did finally take a drag. And once again I coughed like a maniac, confirming to myself that I did not like smoking, but continued to pretend I did. I quickly learned to take tiny puffs without inhaling, just enough to expel the smoke. I did this for all nightclub outings that followed. But with time, I inevitably got comfortable and became used to social smoking. I even graduated to inhaling. That's how it begins.

It's so easy to look back in retrospect and pinpoint when our bad habits began. I became a social smoker, and as the years progressed, a full-fledged one. I discovered I really didn't like menthol cigarettes and became a Du Maurier brand girl. I gave it up a few decades later but started and stopped a few times along the way— as a social smoker—all the while hating that I smoked.

I pride myself on not having an addictive personality. I could shutdown smoking any time. I'll admit, there was still the odd cigarette, especially in stressful times. But if there weren't any cigs around, I wouldn't go into withdrawal, which may have classified me as a social or a stress smoker. But whatever the reason, I should have just said no. No more puffs! Oddly enough, even when I did smoke the odd one, I only smoked half, not wanting to finish. I couldn't tolerate all that smoke going in. And yes, nicotine is addictive. I don't even think nicotine is the worst part of a cigarette, but tar and other *secret* ingredients, like formaldehyde, are definite dangers.

First Real Boyfriend – Kind of

This relationship was a brief interlude that came and went but lingered.

I was seventeen and looking svelte, just newly off that crazy last diet that transformed both my body and my self-esteem. At seventeen I was going to nightclubs, a great social time in my life, and good times were ahead.

A friend of mine was into a guy who waited tables at a restaurant we frequented. He introduced us to his friends, a few of whom had formed a band we eventually went to listen to on Friday nights. During the second visit, Tony the singer and I made some intense eye contact. The chemistry seemed to send electric waves between us.

Tony, as you may well have guessed, was Italian and my first venture into what I thought was *real love*. He introduced me to a new culture of friends, which I enjoyed immensely. I lived for Friday nights, so I could listen to Tony and the band play—and our time together afterward. When I wasn't at the club listening to the band, I'd look forward to Tony's red Dodge Charger pulling up in front of my house to take me on a date, often to our favorite coffee house, where the band members liked to congregate week-day evenings. At the tender age of seventeen, I was sure I'd found my soulmate with this very romantic Italian stud. But what I'd yet to discover was that my Tony was engaged!

Yes, it appeared my old-fashioned Southern-Italian boyfriend was already a marked man for a pre-arranged marriage by his parents. How was I to know? His band had conveniently kept that a big secret from me. But it was one of Tony's *good friends* who spilled the beans. With that devastating news, I broke up with Tony after what seemed a whirlwind romance that only lasted six months. Oh sure, Tony had all the right words—words of love—plus he fessed up and elaborated on the story of his pre-arranged marriage.

Besides the humiliation of being duped and feeling used and questioning myself on what the hell did love mean anyway, my heart was broken. Yet Tony won me over with new promises. I should have learned the first time, but my fantasies of loving a guy so much and knowing instinctively that he loved me, demanded I give him another stupid chance. I hoped that since he came clean and still professed his love for me, he'd cancel the pre-arranged marriage. Lol, I really did live in a fantasy world. But remember, I had nobody to confide in or question about growing up, love, or anything else. I learned life through trial and error, and instincts.

Tony did his best to win back my attention and prove to me I was the love of his life. He invited me to his home to meet his parents, thinking it would prove I was *the one* and demonstrate there was still a chance he would call off the marriage. Wrong! It was wrong on so many levels, but I was sucked in. Eventually, I found my self-respect. I had learned from one of Tony's good friends, who had by then taken an amorous shining to me too, the actual date of the wedding that apparently was still going forward.

I was mortified. I broke it off with Tony. However, because of the circle of friends we shared, it was difficult to avoid bumping into him. But I was conscious of and working diligently on my self-esteem. I would not subject myself to playing second best for anyone. I refused to give Tony the time of day when I'd occasionally see him at the coffeehouse that inevitably became my new hangout.

Early one ironic Saturday early afternoon, I was sitting inside that café sipping on a latte when a shiny black limo, all decorated with paper wedding bells and ribbons, pulled up in front of the window. To this day I still don't know what the purpose of that stop was, but there in the back seat with the window open sat Tony and his new bride. My table near the front window was too close for comfort. Tony and I locked eyes. I shook my head as my gut felt wrenched, and the look on Tony's face when his eyes met mine was so pathetic and full of despair—he didn't look like a happy groom.

Another year would pass until I ran into Tony sitting with his band buddies in the café. He worked hard trying to charm me, as if the passing time would have me forget he lied to me and got married, crushing my heart like a bug. All I could think about was how happy I was that I'd dressed to the nines that day and I was looking mighty fine. I took pleasure in his staring at me while I ignored him. confirming I was someone he'd never have again, despite the torch I knew he still carried for me. By that time, I'd already moved on to a new life and a new man.

Tony appeared off and on in my life at our similar local haunts, because of the friendships I maintained with his fellow band members. It was a good six or seven years before the taint and hurt wore off and I felt I could be friends with him.

One day after those years had passed, Tony caught me sitting alone at the café while I waited for some of my friends to show up. He asked if he could sit down. I pointed to the chair, signaling consent. I was in the prime of my life— looking great, a fulfilling job, and lots of dating. Tony, on the other hand, had developed big bulging dark luggage under his eyes and was halfway to becoming bald. There was no reminiscing, but I felt his loneliness. I kept the conversation to small talk and was fully aware of his sorrowful eyes that seemed to hold much unhappiness. Despite my surmising his situation, I asked him if he was happy. He lamented that letting me go and getting married was the biggest mistake of his life. I concurred and drank up my coffee. I then rose from my chair, slipped on my jacket, and smiled at him as I prepared to leave. He asked when I'd be coming back to the café. I told him his question was irrelevant as he'd made his choice some seven years ago.

My First Apartment

I was nine years old. One last reconciliation between my parents had us moving into the newly developed residential neighborhood. Our big white house with the circular driveway and regal-looking white columns that stood proudly on the front porch was a beautiful sight to take in. A bonus was the path across the street that cut across the park to the playground of our new public school. Our white house, as many referred to it, would be the last home we lived in as a family—longer than in any other home. We lived there for almost nine years. Then a few months shy of my nineteenth birthday, I moved out.

A lifetime of memories was made in that big white house. Many of them don't include my father, who didn't live with us for quite a few of those years. I was sixteen when the final break-up occurred between my parents. And I was already itching to get out of the dysfunction and my mother's rule.

Funny how the times have a way of changing our perspectives. When I look back on that era, compared to nowadays, most kids by their early twenties had moved away from home, and many were already married. I had no aspirations of getting married. By that time in my young life, I'd seen and experienced enough, growing up in a severely broken home.

Within a year after my parents' eventual divorce, Dad decided he couldn't keep a big house and pay rent for himself, so the big white house went up for sale. While I had a difficult time digesting the sale of my only real semblance of a family home, Dad's disclosure of a big surprise gave me something new to look forward to.

During that time, my Aunty Sherry worked for a property management company, and she conveniently was the rental agent for one of the most sought-after apartment complexes in the city for young singles and professionals. People were put on a list and waited a year or more to get one of those coveted apartments. My aunt and father decided that with the sale of the family home, it was time to set me free to build a life and to get me away from my mother's emotional chokehold. It sure helped that my aunt bumped me up to the top of the list.

Dad drove me down to the complex to have a look at my soon-to-be one- bedroom apartment with the sunken living room. I couldn't wait to move in. I'd yet to develop my full-on fearlessness of things. I was still afraid of the dark, but that would be an issue I'd learn to overcome at any price. I was determined to be on my own with no rules, and no badgering from my mother. But some of those aspirations were short-lived. I say this because I could never run far enough to get out of my mother's guilt trips.

Moving day came. My mother had already moved into a rented townhome with my younger siblings, and I was the last one left in our big white house to do a final check around before it closed. My heart sank as I exited my home for the last time, memories of my childhood reeling through my mind, replaying highlights of our family life there for a good chunk of my childhood. I took a last look around, locked the front door, placed the key to the empty house in the mailbox, then jumped into my father's car and took the last load of my belongings to my new home.

It didn't take long for me to bury my sadness for the home and childhood I left behind. When I entered my new home carrying the last boxes from the car, I stood for a moment and inhaled my first breath of freedom. I was excited, standing on the threshold of a new world of living.

I had a good head on my shoulders and didn't look at this move as a time to go crazy with reckless abandon and have wild parties as many a teenager back then had done. I felt at peace, a place to call my own on my own terms with nobody else's rules. Now that's not to say there weren't eventually any parties, but I was self-disciplined. I knew life wasn't a party, and I now had new responsibilities in life. I had to impose my own bedtime curfews so I could get up early in the mornings for work. I had new chores in my own home but had plenty of training from the chores I'd had at home. Cleaning, laundry, and grocery shopping were not new to me. This was my new domain, and everything I'd do from then on became a joy, because I now had my very own place to take care of. And some of the best years of my life were to be had in that apartment.

Besides the bonus of having my aunt working downstairs in the rental office, which gave us loads of opportunity to spend more time together, I'd made several new friends, including my still—best friend of forty years, Zan. We met shortly after I moved in when my aunt got me my part-time job downstairs in the recreation center. Zan worked Saturdays as a lifeguard up at the indoor pool. We had what some would call an *instant connection,* and she opened a world of new friendships and fun. She updated me on life 101. Her friends became my friends, and she taught me the meaning of unconditional love. Despite my being only a few months older than Zan, I felt she was more of a big sister and mother to me. And the passing years have never changed that feeling.

Life was so exciting for the entire twelve years I lived there. I worked hard at growing my low, almost non-existent self-esteem. I read many self-help books, and I had Zan to guide me, stand by me, and raise my self-respect. She filled my heart with love and laughter.

Like all good things, life in my apartment ended when I made a grievous error by leaving and moving in with a man I'd been in a shaky relationship with for a year. I lived, and I learned the hard way, like many young people do who make impulsive decisions. And until I married (someone else) a decade later, those twelve years on my own were the best years of my life.

My First Real Christmas Tree

Ever since I was a young child, I have loved Christmas. The beautiful displays of twinkling lights on the houses, sparkling like jewels in the night, and Santas and reindeer resting on the lawns, would mesmerize me while I'd sit in the backseat of my parents' cars on our way home from somewhere in the night.

Those Christmas trees standing proudly in all their glory, aglow with their varied colored lights illuminating the darkness of cold winter, had my imagination soaring with thoughts of more beautiful trees that sat inside people's homes brightening up rooms, stacked below with beautifully wrapped gift boxes for children to open on Christmas day. Toys, dolls, games. How exciting to be part of such a sparkly and joyous event, gathered round the tree with hot cocoa in hand, singing carols, and celebrating the magic of Christmas.

We didn't have a Christmas tree, not for the lack of my pestering my mother about why we couldn't have a beautiful tree like some of my friends had. "Jewish people don't have Christmas trees," she announced with authority. But I had an answer for everything. I continued the badgering, asking why then we couldn't have a Hannukah bush? I was determined to have some sort of tree with sparkly lights in my home. I wanted Santa to visit our house too and bring us presents. I never stopped asking as each new Christmas season approached.

Religion confused me for most of my growing-up years. We only celebrated the *high holidays*, and always at my paternal grandparents' home. They were devout religious Jews, yet we only adhered to their strict religious laws while in their home. We had little education on what those holidays represented. Religion wasn't a big topic of conversation in my family. Whatever I'd learned was during my young Sunday school days, where instruction focused on the *children's version* of Jewish holidays. To be honest, I found Catholic holidays much more fun and exciting.

The story of Hannukah fascinated me when I learned about the miracle of the oil that burned for eight days and nights. The Jews hid from prosecution in the temple with a lamp that was meant to burn only for one day but lasted for eight. I learned the most about Passover holiday by watching *The*

Ten Commandments on TV many times throughout my childhood. One thing this movie taught me was why we ate unleavened bread during the Pharaoh's reign. But none of our holidays seemed as exciting as Christmas. On Hannukah we received money as a gift, and I need not explain how unexciting that was for a child. I wanted sparkly lights and presents. I wanted the burly man in a red suit who slipped down other children's chimneys to visit my home too.

Religion was confusing to me because on weekdays at home we lived like everyone else. We ate bacon. Dad loved ordering Chinese food and pizza. At my grandparents' home where I'd spent most of my childhood on weekends, no pork allowed. Just the mention of it was enough to send my grandparents off the rails, despite their knowing we didn't live their way in our home. It was a confusing childhood to say the least, but despite my confusion, my determination to be a part of Christmas never faltered.

Being the eldest child with a vivid imagination, I'd tell my younger siblings stories about Christmas. I'd convince them there was a Santa by telling them stories I'd learned from friends at school. And by the time I was ten years old, I had us all hanging up a sock over the fireplace on Christmas Eve. We may not have had the tree, but we had a fireplace, and that meant there was still a chance Santa may pop by. I'd saved some of my allowance to buy candies and various treats to put in each of my sibling's stockings, ensuring they too believed in Santa.

By the time I moved away from home, my desire to have my first very own Christmas tree came to fruition. And as inexperienced as I was with Christmas tree care, I learned after my first one.

When someone feels deprived of something most of their life, I think the feeling intensifies until they finally get the chance to fulfil their desires. At least that's how it was for me. I wanted a massive Christmas tree. The bigger the better. I had no idea that once trees thawed out and opened their branches, they were much larger. I also learned never again to buy a Scotch Pine with their sharp and menacing needles that liked to fall and get lost in my blue shag rug.

I may also have gone a tad overboard when buying decorations, and I may have forgotten to water my tree—okay, maybe for a few days in a row. And I certainly didn't give a thought to how I was ever going to remove the tree once the season was over—a season I may have extended into late January as I stalled taking down the tree. But as that big Scotch Pine grew bare, needles falling and limbs spreading out humongously, taking up one-third of my living room space, the time had finally come for removal.

The day had come to round up a few friends to help me remove the tree. The thought of moving it through my apartment to the front door scared me. I imagined the remainder of dried-up needles being shaken off and embedding themselves into my shag rug. But, as luck would have it, my living room window could handle the task. My two friends and I did our best wrapping garbage bags around the tree as we folded in the branches and taped it up. We struggled to lift it but finally got it high enough to chuck out the window. Then we made a mad dash down to the parking lot where it landed and put the remains in the nearby dumpster. What a job! But it was so worth it. And so began the ritual I would practice every year. Eventually, as the decades would pass, I learned to love imitation Christmas trees. They served the same purpose with less mess.

From Blonde to Wrong

The curiosity leads many girls to search for their identity by trying out fresh new looks—haircuts, hair color, and style. Most of us growing up are unhappy with our God-given attributes, and some of us are curious enough to see how we feel with a new look. Back in my heydays, it seemed all the girls wanted to be blonde. But for me, as I approached my mid-twenties, I became bored with my natural blonde hair color and tired of the abuse I gave it by adding blonder highlights. No longer impressed by the *Je ne sais quoi* I enjoyed for years, I now craved something daring to complement my bold personality I'd worked so hard to develop on my journey to building self-esteem. I finally summoned the courage. It was time to become a redhead. The only decision left to make was what shade of red to choose.

Don't get me wrong, this decision was in no way impulsive. I'd hemmed and hawed over changing up things for almost a year before settling on a shade and drumming up the courage to go forth and create. I'd weighed the pros and cons of how light or bright to go, and I delighted in the thought of the fringe benefits of going red. Besides my bold decision to do a drastic makeover, I also thought about the money I'd save by not doing my highlights every few months and, of course, how the abuse to my hair would ease. No more tinfoil-wrapped hair in icky peroxide concoction. Yes. Red was going to be the new blonde for me. At that time, I didn't know many redheads and my goal was originality. I was already well-preened with fashion and my skincare regimen, and after checking my skin tone against several sample swatches, I was ready to pull off becoming a redhead—something not all women can do successfully, mostly because one cannot judge the color outcome by looking at a drugstore box of hair dye, and because carrying off red hair properly has a lot to do with natural skin tones. Red can be a major clash with natural skin tone, so I would always recommend going to a salon to have a drastic color change done properly.

So, there I was, standing in the hair dye aisle of my local pharmacy, scouting out colors and brands, and scrutinizing the backs of boxes for diagrams and hair color charts. I studied those charts . . . *if your base color is A, your hair will look like B.* Would

I ever go by those examples again? Hell no. But, back then, I'd made my decision. I knew my skin tone could pull off red hair without making me look gaunt and artificial, so I chose the beautiful shade of deep cherry. I thought it would do me justice and transform me into a fiery redhead. I couldn't wait to get back home and begin the transformation.

I'd never colored my own hair, so I read the instructions thoroughly and took another look at the color chart. The lighter my base color was, the redder my hair would become. My blonde base was the best place to start with because of how light it was, so I assumed it would grab the color quickly—or so I thought. I also anticipated my lighter blonde streaks would retain a highlighted effect of intermingled red and redder locks. What could go wrong?

It was almost too easy. All I did was add the tube of color to the contents in the plastic bottle, shake it up, put on the plastic gloves, and squirt it all over my hair. Ten minutes later, my once blonde mane was covered in deep red dye. I set the timer and filled the half-hour wait time by looking through my makeup to find palettes of eyeshadow that would play nice with my new hair color- to-be. I decided a change from the green and blue eyeshadows I usually wore would do better with a more muted palette of brown and peach tones to neutralize my new bold hair color. The time was almost up when I peeked in the mirror and became a tad concerned with the new darkness crowning on my head, but I wasn't too alarmed as I knew everything wet seemed darker.

My relief was short-lived. I rinsed out the dye, conditioned my hair, wrapped it in a towel, then sat down at my vanity table to apply makeup, preparing for my new dramatic look. Only my new *do* became a resounding *don't*.

I removed the towel from my head, shook out my hair, then reached below my cabinet underneath the sink and retrieved the blow dryer. I began drying my strands when the horror struck me. I screamed. My hair was by no means red! It looked such a dark mahogany that it appeared almost black. I plopped myself down on the toilet seat and sobbed uncontrollably. I continued to shout out loud, *what have I done?* I wasn't some inexperienced teenager. I was twenty-five years of age with a good head on my shoulders—or at least it was a good head before I became someone I didn't recognize. That's what I got for taking on the monumental task of changing hair color on my own and not going to a professional to ease me into the transition.

After my initial meltdown and when I finally regained my composure, I realized I'd created a mess and was now in dire need of a professional to help to lighten the dark mass of hair I was sporting—a major clash with my skin tone. Humiliated, I picked up the phone and called my hairdresser. I'd been with Edith for years and even graduated from going to the salon to being invited to have my hair done at her home. I kicked myself for not calling her first to ask pertinent questions before diving into a potential disaster. But I summoned the courage and in between sobs, shared my hair nightmare as I listened to her scold me for diving into such a drastic color change without her expert help. Apparently, I missed some steps in preparing for the color change, especially when going from porous blonde to a darker color. All I remember Edith shouting at me was that it was important for my blonde highlights to be treated first with a darker blonde base toner. This color game had rules and was supposed to be done in steps, leaving a few days of breathing room between the processes. Thankfully, Edith invited me to scoot over to her house to begin the repair—and for the lecture about dying hair and how to prepare. What a fiasco for both me and my poor hair. I was petrified that all my hair would fall out from the color abuse.

Edith first stripped out all the mahogany dye with peroxide. She then toned down the albino-looking pigmentless hair with an ashen shade of toner, which would prepare my hair for the darker color. Turns out the color chart on the box of hair dye I'd purchased was based on *if your hair is naturally this color* . . . Natural, being the operative word I overlooked because, for so many years, I'd interspersed platinum highlights with my own golden blonde shade and felt my color was *natural*. Duh me!

Once Edith finished with me for the day, I looked human again, although not thrilled about the new ashy shade of blonde she'd turned me into. She informed me how badly abused my hair had been from all the dying and stripping, and that I should leave it alone for a week or so to give my sore scalp rest. Then I was to return, and she'd make me a proper redhead.

Thirty plus some odd years later, I'm still a redhead, albeit a few variations of red through the decades, but never dark, and never again from a drugstore brand. Yes, I do still dye my own hair, only my bottle of red comes from the beauty supply. Hey, I'm like a pro now. I'm a fast study. I learn quickly after a disaster.

First Loss of a Friend – When Friends Die

First times aren't always celebratory, especially when it applies to death.

By the time I'd reached my mid-forties, I could count on two hands the number of loved ones to whom I'd already said goodbye—my father, my aunt, three uncles, and all remaining grandparents. I dealt with and accepted the passing differently with each one I'd loved and lost. Losing a parent, child, sibling, spouse, or a friend affects each loved one left behind with an individual sadness all its own. But though experiencing various types of grief, I hadn't yet lost a close friend. This was a new kind of bereavement. Learning that a friend who was the same age as me could die while still so young, felt too close to home.

We tagged ourselves the three amigas—my best friend Bri, Al (short for Alba), and me. I'd met Al through Bri shortly after Bri and I became friends in the early 80s. Until meeting Al, I thought I was the one with the loudest personality and utmost chutzpah, but Al was a force to be reckoned with. She had a comeback for every indignation, and only kindness and a giant smile for everyone else. She was a hard-headed Southern-Italian beauty who could cook up a storm at a moment's notice and lift anyone's spirits with her wit, humor, and kind-heartedness. She was a master at sneaking out of her house to escape her dominating husband when Bri and I coaxed her to join us for an outing to a café or for some girl time at one of our homes.

Alba was loud and beautiful. She was a real knockout and, no matter where we were in public, men always turned to take a second look. I'm sure her magnetism was a big part of her husband's fear of losing her. He harbored an excessive and unhealthy distrust. Al didn't even have a driver's license because her husband wouldn't allow her to go anywhere without him. Snatching her up and sneaking her out of the house was always a major accomplishment.

Al had a luxurious mane of thick, pitch-black hair she wore down to her waist. Her demeanor exuded sexy. She was tall, dark, and stunning. Her olive and sun-kissed complexion, alluring dark eyes, and natural full lips (that women would pay big bucks to have)—together with her sharp wit and kind heart—made Al a beautiful soul, inside and out. I don't think the girl had ever had to worry about dieting, as she was naturally tall and lanky. I don't recall anything she ever ate putting an ounce on her.

The three of us hung out together at each other's homes, mostly on Bri's front veranda in summer; but my apartment was often the great sanctuary and getaway for them since both were in unhappy marriages. We held parties at my place (me being the only single one in the group), went dancing at nightclubs (which was real magic for Al when she was able to pull off getting out of the house), and spent many a weekend or evening hanging out at our favorite Italian café. There was never a dull moment when Al was around, and no shortage of male attention.

Our twenties were the good years, filled with lots of fun moments and memories. It seems all we did was laugh whenever we were together. Eventually, like everything else in life, things changed for all of us. Bri divorced, I moved away from our neighborhood, and Al finally made her wish come true by divorcing her husband. Bri and I remained besties, but Al got busy experiencing life with her newfound freedom, as her strict upbringing and marrying young left her craving all the single life had to offer.

Bri and I kept in touch with her, but like what usually happens when someone takes a new path and finds romance, Al's social life grew exponentially as she explored new avenues, dating, and eventually a new boyfriend. Bri and I also entered new relationships, but we were tight.

Ten years passed before Al resurfaced in my and Bri's lives. Al was happy and secure in a new relationship with her live-in boyfriend in her new home. And after doing some catching up on fun and freedom and living, couples began getting together. Al now lived in the same vicinity as me. Once downtown girls, we now were uptown girls with settled lives. Our friendship picked up exactly from where it had left off. Al was content, in love, and beaming with happiness in her new life. The only thing that changed was she wasn't as forthright—especially about the part of her cancer diagnosis.

Even during her prison-like marriage, Al was no complainer and could crack a joke a minute. But sometimes she joked around about her *damned leg* that suddenly would give out on her. If she complained it was always with humor and the distinguished wide-grinning smile, which never, ever left her face. She began dropping subtle comments in gest, as she'd tell me her leg would sometimes become dead weight for a moment, then she'd be fine. For as long as I knew Al, she'd never been sick, not even a cold that I could remember. She'd laugh while telling me about her *stupid* leg, making fun of herself, repeating over and over what a klutz she was. But after hearing about her leg problem too many times, I begged her to go to the doctor and get a test. She finally did.

After a few months, Al dropped by less often. When I'd call to check up on her, she didn't reveal much. She kept telling me she was having more tests done. I hadn't seen her for a while, so I stopped by her house one day. That's when I saw my sparkly, effervescent friend in a wheelchair. My heart sank. "WTF is going on?" I shrieked. And that was the day Al finally spilled the beans with no fear, pure optimism, saying she had a tumor on her spine. She laid out the details about all the tests she had done and her upcoming surgery. The doctors would remove the tumor and she'd be out of that chair in no time. That's what she told me. And I believed her.

Alba was the most optimistic person I'd ever known. Determined to conquer any obstacle, she never showed fear and demanded no pity. I went along with her optimism. The doctors had informed her they may not be able to remove the entire tumor because it was too near the spinal cord, and they didn't want to paralyze her for life. My stoic friend had the surgery and, no, they couldn't remove the whole tumor, so she did the necessary radiation and chemo to hopefully eradicate the residual tumor and continue living life with her joyful as always disposition.

Every time I spoke with or visited Al, she'd laugh as always and tell more stories about her crazy pre-tumor adventures. My life was busy, and Al was busy fighting for her life. Our phone calls became less frequent. Al's two young girls occupied her time between treatments and doctors' appointments, and I had recently moved into a new home. But when we finally did catch up, we gabbed and laughed as we always had, with barely a mention of her situation and prognosis. She wanted it that way, and I didn't want to break her spirit. She assured me she was on the road to recovery. That was good enough for me. Then a few days after our last call, one of her sisters phoned to inform me Alba had gone into a hospice.

My heart aches all over again while I relive the memory of my good friend Alba and the gut-wrenching news. I had planned on visiting her the very next day, but Bri called and told me she'd just gotten *the call* from Al's youngest daughter. My beautiful friend was taken.

Alba did everything on her own terms. The light of hope always shone from her eyes, even when purposely deceiving her friends, because she never wanted to be a burden to anyone. She didn't want to burst anyone's balloon of hope—even when she knew her own fate.

I hung up the phone and cried my heart out for hours. The hurt in my heart was palpable. I spent the evening reminiscing about the younger and better days of our friendship. So many memories faded to black as I realized there would be no more memories made between me and my good friend Al.

A few days later, Bri and I made our way to the cemetery together. Al was laid to rest inside the marbled walls of a mausoleum. Bri and I held each other's hands tight as our grief bubbled within our broken hearts and endless pools of tears continued to fall from our eyes.

That day, mortality hit me hard. Al was the first friend I'd lost to death, leaving me feeling much too close to its finality. Death has no age limits I knew this, but I certainly never knew how it would feel to lose a friend at a young age. Death doesn't bypass the kind-hearted, a single mother of two young girls, or those who go to church regularly. Death can choose whomever it wants, leaving behind a great gaping hole in the hearts of those who loved and lost and were left behind in its wake. Losing a good friend hit me hard. Alba was too young and too beautiful to die.

It was sobering. How dare death have the gumption to snatch my friend away just when she finally began to make her happiness. The audacity of death plagues me.

Epilogue – Almost

I can't help but wonder if my fifteen first times were my compass in life, setting up the direction for whom and how I'd become me, and leading to the paths I'd choose forward. I learned exactly how that old saying about doors really does ring true—the choices we make in life are derived from the sum of our experiences, essential components to what sets and moves us forward in life.

When we're young we're more curious than cautious, and as we age, our accrued wisdom becomes our guide to the future choices we make. Looking back at the chapters in this book, I see my growth in stages. Initially, it was my fears of growth that held me back from doing many things in my teen years because I didn't have a comfort bond with anyone who could make me eager enough to share feelings and questions—save for my maternal Aunty Sherry, although I remained cautious about approaching her with some of my personal concerns, because

I knew her first allegiance was to her sister, my mother.

My *crimson tide* humiliation taught me that if I ever had a daughter, I would teach her about *the birds and the bees* before she'd have to face the frightening moment alone without knowledge about what was happening with her body. As for the crazy diets, it would have been nice to have learned that going on diets and losing weight doesn't mean the journey is over. There is a lifestyle of maintenance and good eating habits to follow to maintain weight loss.

Kissing and love are a part of life, and each of us must endeavor to learn about the joy and pain of loving. Sure, it would be nice if our parents gave us a heads up about how hearts get smitten when the lovebug bites. But ultimately, we cannot grow from love unless we experience the highs and lows of relationships for ourselves.

My big European vacation taught me many lessons about life—friendship, flirting, culture, how ridiculous I must have looked wearing four-inch spikes in the desert, consequences for not obeying laws, and how much my father had spoiled me.

Death evokes a different level of grief for everyone left behind. When my paternal grandmother died, I had no tears to shed until I saw my father cry and it broke my heart to pieces. When my paternal grandfather died, I cried for the devastation left behind for me and my siblings in the aftermath. When my Aunty Sherry died, a few years before my father, the pain and grief I felt was worse than any I had yet experienced. I felt I had lost my mother. My father's death left a searing hole in my heart that is still raw today, thirty-one years later. And losing a best friend presented a whole new level of grief, one that hit close to home and scared the hell out me. If death can claim someone who has her whole life ahead of her, then no one is invincible. When it comes to death, everyone is fair game.

But mostly, I have no regrets about my life—mistakes, bad decisions, and all. If it weren't for trial and error, diving into unchartered waters, and doing ridiculous things, we wouldn't learn or have anything to compare. Hindsight gives us insight. I could say it would have been nice to have the had foresight during actual events, but how fun would that have been? We must experience the bumps along the journey to appreciate where we land. Only then can we look back and gauge how far we've come.

Life lessons leave an indelible imprint on who we are, what we do, and the path we take forward. If we don't learn and grow, we're forced to repeat the lessons until we do.

First and Last Love – A Tribute to My Beloved Husband

Life, love, and laughter.

Humor. It's the one thing that always got me through some of the darker moments in life. The first real love of my life was my husband. I like to say I married him because he made me laugh, but the truth is, it was so much more than that. With him I learned the true meaning of what true unconditional love means—something I'd never felt in my entire life with any other man.

Until I met my husband, no other man could make me laugh. In fact, laughter was my pathway through life. Being a self-conscious child, teen, and young adult, I had made it my business to be a funny girl, because laughter could mask so many scars, aches, and insecurities. I felt my flaws as I grew, and I learned from a young age that if I could make people laugh with me, it may deter them from laughing at me.

As the years passed and I learned how to grow self-esteem and feel proud of myself, I no longer worried about being laughed at. And as I came into myself, I learned I was actually a funny girl with a great sense of humor, and I realized I no longer had to use humor as camouflage. It just was. My sense of humor grew with me, and no longer had to compensate for my flaws.

I was the funny one in my circles. I'd say that in most of my romantic relationships, it was my good sense of humor that attracted men. And deep down inside, no matter people's issues, they loved to laugh. But it was always me making someone else laugh. It was as though I always found men who were somehow broken, despite their profession or successes or standing in society. That was until I met my husband. Here was a man who made *me* laugh—every single day of our lives together.

Other than some good times and particular incidents that were funny in other relationships, I hadn't experienced laughter every day with anyone until I met my husband. For the first time in my life, I laughed daily in a relationship. Even if something got me down, my G would always remind me of the brighter side of life and encourage me to remember the much bigger things we had. Sure, he had his share of ups and downs like anybody else, but he had a special way of getting through and past those things. He didn't dwell on past wounds, and he wasn't a broken man.

My G was the first true love of my life. He loved me through all my war wounds unconditionally. We laughed our way through hard times and shared a most beautiful life together. That was until God put a stop to it and decided to take him for himself.

He became very ill after I completed the first draft of this book, and I let the book sit and collect cobwebs throughout that journey and into the next one full of grief. He was the greatest love and loss of my life.

When he left me, I felt the laughter in me go with him. I mourn the loss of him daily, hourly, and with every breath I still take. My first steps into this life without him find me trying to learn how to make my way back to the world of the living. My heart is shattered, but the laughter still lives within me every time I think of his many inspirational sayings, his beautiful smile, and the life we shared together that will always reside in my heart.

My G was my very first true love, and he will always remain the last greatest love of my life.

About the Author

D.G. Kaye is a Canadian author living in Toronto, Canada. She writes nonfiction and memoirs about her life experiences, matters of the heart, and self-help about women's issues. Her positive outlook keeps D.G. on track, allowing her to take on life's challenges with a dose of humor in her quest to overcome adversity.

D.G. began writing when pen and paper became the tools to express her pent-up emotions during her turbulent childhood. She began journaling about her life at a young age and continued writing about the imprints and lessons she learned through people and events she encountered. D.G. writes books to share her stories and inspiration. She advocates for kindness and for women's empowerment. Her favorite saying is "For every kindness received, there should be kindness in return. Wouldn't that just make the world right?"

When she's not writing, D.G. loves to read (self-help books and stories of triumph), cook (concocting new recipes, never to come out the same way twice), shop (only if it's a great sale), play poker (when she gets the chance), and, most of all, travel.

Visit D.G.'s Author Pages:

www.amazon.com/author/dgkaye7
www.goodreads.com/dgkaye

Contact D.G. at:

author@dgkayewriter.com

Follow D.G. on her Social Sites:

www.twitter.com/@pokercubster
www.facebook.com/dgkaye
www.linkedin.com/in/dgkaye7

Visit D.G.'s new Podcast –
Grief, the Real Talk

https://www.youtube.com/debbyDGKayeGies

Other Books by D.G. Kaye

P.S. I Forgive You – A Broken Legacy

Purchase link:

www.smarturl.it/bookPSIForgiveYou

"I hurt for her. She wasn't much of a mother, but she was still my mother."

Confronted with resurfacing feelings of guilt, D.G. Kaye is tormented by her decision to remain estranged from her dying emotionally abusive mother after resolving to banish her years ago, an event she has shared in her book *Conflicted Hearts*. In *P.S. I Forgive You*, Kaye takes us on a compelling heartfelt journey as she seeks to understand the roots of her mother's narcissism, let go of past hurts, and find forgiveness for both her mother and herself.

After struggling for decades to break free, Kaye has severed the unhealthy ties that bound her to her dominating mother—but now Kaye battles new confliction, as the guilt she harbors over her decision only increases as the end of her mother's life draws near. Kaye once again struggles with her conscience and her feelings of being obligated to return to a painful past she thought she left behind.

Excerpt – Aftermath

My mother is dead.

She had been dying for so many years that when the day finally came, my heart was drowning in a swirling abyss of guilt. The years of emotional turmoil I had pent up as the daughter of a narcissistic mother had reached their denouement.

My anger and past resentment toward my mother had turned into an inquisition, a searching of my soul. I needed to understand the root of her ego. It was not enough for me to lay her body to rest. I needed to fill in the gaps, find out what had spurred the injustices she inflicted on so many, and clear the debris lingering in my own conscience to make peace with my past and send her off with my forgiveness.

I had realized how emotionally toxic it was to hang on to hurt and resentment, but the death of my emotionally abusive mother didn't necessarily end the residual hurt of being abused. To set my heart free, I needed to seek out a path to resolve past hurts and the conflict that had tainted my memories.

I'll never know if peace waits for my mother on the other side. I wonder if the afterlife offers second chances to wrongdoers or if they learn lessons from the injustices they commit while on earth. I'd like to think God has mercy and has welcomed my mother into heaven with the same forgiveness

I have granted her after learning to surrender my resentments. Looking back, I have realized what a lost soul my mother really was.

Through all her theatrics, lies, and betrayals as she portrayed herself as the person she wanted to be, or perhaps believed she was, my mother harbored a damaged soul that didn't know how to dig itself out. The same persona she had created to shine in the limelight, to acquire anything she desired, or to disguise her insecurities ironically became her downfall.

This story is the aftermath, my way of coming to terms with and relinquishing the guilt and instilled fears I have carried from childhood. It is my decision to banish my mother from my life and a resolution to find peace within myself with my decision.

Conflicted Hearts

A Daughter's Quest for Solace from Emotional Guilt

Purchase link:
www.smarturl.it/bookconflictedhearts

*"**Somehow I believed it was my obligation to try to do the right thing by her because she had given birth to me.**"*

Burdened with constant worry for her father and the guilt caused by her mother's narcissism, D.G. Kaye had a short childhood. When she moved away from home at eighteen, she began to grow into herself, overcoming her lack of guidance and her insecurities.

Her life experiences became her teachers, and she learned from the mistakes and choices she made along the way, plagued by the guilt she carried for her mother.

Conflicted Hearts is a heartfelt journey of self-discovery and acceptance, an exploration of the quest for solace from emotional guilt.

Words We Carry

Essays of Obsession and Self-Esteem

Purchase link:
www.smarturl.it/bookwordswecarry

"I have been a great critic of myself for most of my life, and I was darned good at it, deflating my own ego without the help of anyone else."

What do our shopping habits, high-heeled shoes, and big hair have to do with how we perceive ourselves? Do the slights we endured when we were young affect how we choose our relationships now? D.G. takes us on a journey, unlocking the hurts of the past by identifying situations that hindered her own self-esteem. Her anecdotes and confessions demonstrate how the hurtful events in our lives linger and set the tone for how we value our own self-worth. *Words We Carry* is a raw, personal accounting of how the author overcame the demons of low self-esteem with the determination to learn to love herself.

~~~

MenoWhat? A Memoir
Memorable Moments of Menopause

Purchase ink:
www.smarturl.it/bookMenoWhatAMemoir

"I often found myself drifting from a state of normal in a sudden twist of bitchiness."

From PMS to menopause to what the hell?

D.G. adds a touch of humor to a tale about a not-so-humorous time. While bidding farewell to her dearly departing estrogen, D.G. struggles to tame her raging hormones of fire, relentless dryness, flooding and droughts and other unflattering symptoms.

Join D.G. on her meno-journey to slay the dragons of menopause as she tries to hold on to her sanity, memory, hair, and so much more!

Have Bags, Will Travel
Trips and Tales: Memoirs of an Over-packer
Purchase link:
www.smarturl.it/bookHaveBags

D.G. Kaye is back, and as she reflects on some of her more memorable vacations and travel snags, she finds herself constantly struggling to keep one step ahead of the ever-changing guidelines of the airlines—with her overweight luggage in tow. Her stories alert us to some of the pitfalls of being an obsessive shopper, especially when it comes time for D.G. to bring her treasures home, and remind us of the simpler days when traveling was a breeze.

In her quest to keep from tipping the scales, D.G. strives to devise new tricks to fit everything in her suitcases on each trip. Why is she consistently a target for Canada customs on her return journeys?

D.G.'s witty tales take us from airports, to travel escapades with best friends, to reflections on how time can change the places we hold dear in our hearts. Her memories will entertain and have you reminiscing about some of your own most treasured journeys—and perhaps make you contemplate revamping your packing strategies.

Twenty Years: After "I Do"

Reflections on Love
and Changes Through Aging

May/December memoirs.

In this personal accounting, D.G. Kaye shares the insights and wisdom she has accrued through twenty years of keeping her marriage strong and thriving despite the everyday changes and challenges of aging. Kaye reveals how a little creative planning, acceptance, and unconditional love can create a bond no obstacle will break. Kaye's stories are informative, inspiring, and a testament to love eclipsing all when two people understand, respect, and honor their vows. She adds that a daily sprinkling of laughter is a staple in nourishing a healthy marriage.

Twenty years began with a promise. As Kaye recounts what transpired within that time, she shows that true love has no limits, even when one spouse ages ahead of the other.

Universal link:
http://www.smarturl.it/bookTwentyYearsAfter